Contents

W9-BDM-616

How to Use This Book 2
Skills Correlation Guide 3

Pre-assessment Activities
Whole Numbers: Place Value 4
Addition and Subtraction:
   Addition 5
Multiplication and Division:
   Multiplication 6
Fractions: Finding Fractions 7
Decimals: Decimals and
   Fractions 8
Money: Dollars and Cents 9

Whole Numbers
Teaching Tips 10
Place Value: How Many Miles? ... 11
Ordering Numbers:
   Put Them in Order 12
Rounding Numbers:
   Tens and Hundreds 13
Rounding Numbers:
   Rounding Up or Down 14
Post-assessment Activities 15

Addition and Subtraction
Teaching Tips 16
Addition: Number Problems 17
Addition: Word Problems 18
Subtraction: Number Problems .. 19
Subtraction: Word Problems 20
Post-assessment Activities 21

Multiplication and Division
Teaching Tips 22
Multiplication:
   Number Problems 23
Multiplication: So Many Birds! .. 24
Division: Number Problems 25
Division: Remainders 26
Post-assessment Activities 27

Fractions
Teaching Tips 28
Adding and Subtracting
   Fractions: Finding Fractions ... 29
Adding and Subtracting
   Fractions: Plus or Minus 30
Mixed Numbers:
   How Much Do You Need? 31
Percentages: America's People ... 32
Post-assessment Activities 33

Decimals
Teaching Tips 34
Decimals and Fractions:
   Matching the Fraction 35
Addition and Subtraction:
   Adding and Subtracting
   Decimals 36
Decimals and Mixed Numbers:
   Decimals Greater Than 1 37
Addition and Subtraction:
   Adding and Subtracting
   Decimals Greater Than 1 38
Post-assessment Activities 39

Money
Teaching Tips 40
Decimals: Using Decimals
   to Write Money Amounts 41
Dollars and Cents: Greater
   Than, Less Than, or Equal To? .. 42
Addition: Shopping at
   the Farmers' Market 43
Subtraction: Shopping at
   the Bookstore 44
Post-assessment Activities 45

Answer Key 46

How to Use This Book

The activities in *Numbers and Operations* are meant to help learners master third-grade mathematics skills. *Numbers and Operations* focuses on developing skills such as place value, addition, subtraction, working with decimals, and recognizing money value. These curricula-based activities and skills follow the National Council of Teachers of Mathematics (NCTM) standards.

Numbers and Operations is organized into six sections: Whole Numbers, Addition and Subtraction, Multiplication and Division, Fractions, Decimals, and Money.

Whole Numbers

In this section, learners will strengthen their understanding of large numbers through activities that focus on place value up to the thousands place and ordering numbers in the thousands. Learners will also practice rounding numbers to the nearest 10, 100, and 1,000.

Addition and Subtraction

Learners will develop their addition and subtraction skills by solving number and word problems that involve numbers up to four places.

Multiplication and Division

The activities in this section will give learners practice in multiplication and division as they solve both number and word problems.

Fractions

Learners will use the activities in this section to develop their ability to work with fractions. The activities focus on adding and subtracting fractions and mixed numbers as well as percentages and fractions.

Decimals

In this section, learners strengthen their understanding of decimals through activities that focus on adding and subtracting decimals less than one and decimals greater than one.

Money

The activities in this section help learners understand the relationship between decimals and money. Learners also gain practice in recognizing money values and adding and subtracting amounts of money.

Skills Correlation Guide

	Number Sense	Computation	Percentages	Rounding Numbers	Word Problems	Calculating Decimals	Mixed Numbers	Comparing Numbers	Recognizing Money	Place Value	Adding	Subtraction	Decimal and Fraction Equivalent
Whole Numbers (pp. 11–15)	✓			✓				✓		✓			
Addition and Subtraction (pp. 17–21)	✓	✓			✓						✓	✓	
Multiplication and Division (pp. 23–27)	✓				✓								
Fractions (pp. 29–33)	✓	✓	✓		✓		✓				✓	✓	
Decimals (pp. 35–39)	✓	✓			✓	✓	✓			✓	✓	✓	✓
Money (pp. 41–45)	✓	✓			✓	✓		✓	✓	✓	✓	✓	

The activities featured in this book are level N according to the guidelines set by Fountas and Pinnell.

© Rosen School Supply•Brain Builders Numbers and Operations•3•RSS-8572-5

Name _____

Place Value

👉 **Directions: The trucks below have to deliver books every day. Write the number of books in the space provided.**

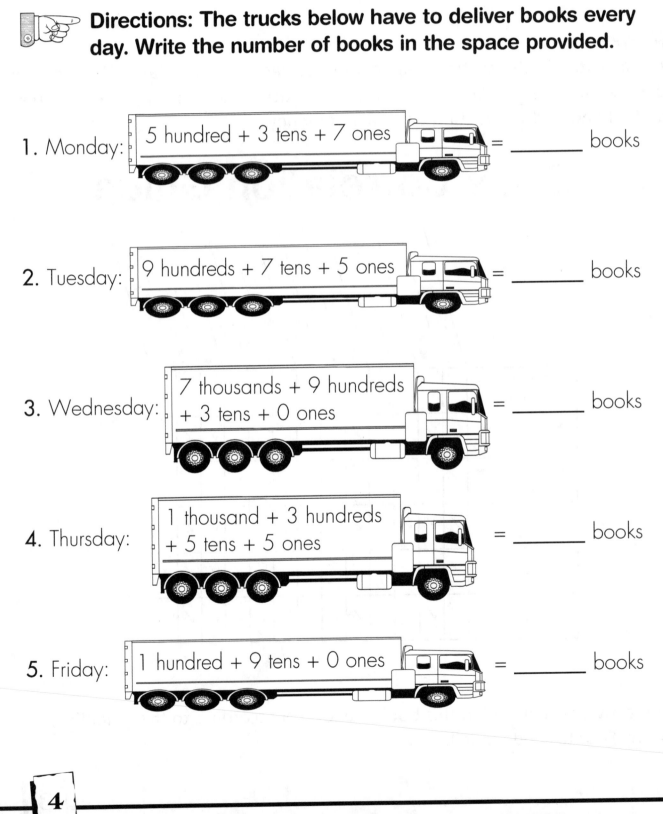

1. Monday: | 5 hundred + 3 tens + 7 ones | = _____ books

2. Tuesday: | 9 hundreds + 7 tens + 5 ones | = _____ books

3. Wednesday: | 7 thousands + 9 hundreds + 3 tens + 0 ones | = _____ books

4. Thursday: | 1 thousand + 3 hundreds + 5 tens + 5 ones | = _____ books

5. Friday: | 1 hundred + 9 tens + 0 ones | = _____ books

Name _____

Addition

👉 **Directions: Solve the following word problems with addition.**

1. Cindy is helping her mother plan a picnic. Her grandparents, aunts, uncles, and cousins are all going to be there. Cindy and her mother decided they would need 35 hamburgers and 68 hot dogs. How many hamburgers and hot dogs will they need altogether?

   _____

2. Greg had 142 stamps in his stamp collection. His sister, Sue, gave him 17 stamps to add to his collection. Then his dad gave him 12 more stamps. How many stamps does Greg have now?

   _____

3. Christina stops at the market to buy flowers three times a week. On Monday, she bought 12 red roses. On Wednesday, she got 24 white daisies. On Saturday, she picked up 30 lilies. How many flowers did Christina buy for the week?

   _____

4. The We'll Paint Your House Company painted 144 houses last year. This year the company painted 200 houses. How many houses has the company painted in the last two years?

   _____

Name _____

Multiplication

👉 **Directions: Solve the problems using multiplication.**

1. $\begin{array}{r} 17 \\ \times\ 5 \\ \hline \end{array}$

2. $\begin{array}{r} 6 \\ \times\ 3 \\ \hline \end{array}$

3. $\begin{array}{r} 90 \\ \times\ 2 \\ \hline \end{array}$

4. $\begin{array}{r} 14 \\ \times\ 8 \\ \hline \end{array}$

5. $\begin{array}{r} 25 \\ \times\ 5 \\ \hline \end{array}$

6. $\begin{array}{r} 8 \\ \times\ 7 \\ \hline \end{array}$

7. $\begin{array}{r} 32 \\ \times\ 2 \\ \hline \end{array}$

8. $\begin{array}{r} 12 \\ \times\ 4 \\ \hline \end{array}$

9. $\begin{array}{r} 10 \\ \times\ 3 \\ \hline \end{array}$

Name _____

Finding Fractions

 Directions: Add or subtract the fractions. Then color in the fraction of each shape that represents your answer.

1. $\dfrac{2}{4} + \dfrac{1}{4} = \underline{}\,_4$

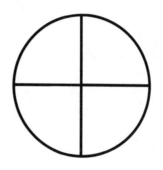

2. $\dfrac{5}{9} + \dfrac{2}{9} = \underline{}\,_9$

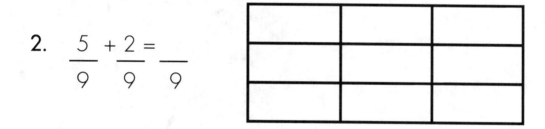

3. $\dfrac{3}{5} - \dfrac{2}{5} = \underline{}\,_5$

4. $\dfrac{8}{8} - \dfrac{4}{8} = \underline{}\,_8$

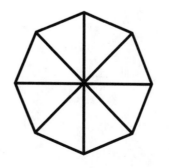

© Rosen School Supply•Brain Builders Numbers and Operations•3•RSS-8572-5

Name _____

Decimals and Fractions

👉 **Directions: Draw a line from the decimal to the fraction that matches it.**

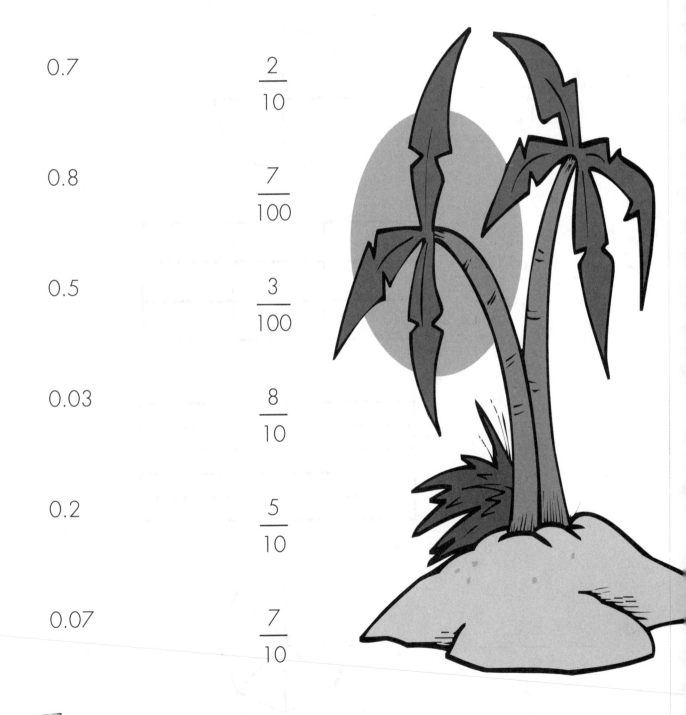

0.7	$\dfrac{2}{10}$
0.8	$\dfrac{7}{100}$
0.5	$\dfrac{3}{100}$
0.03	$\dfrac{8}{10}$
0.2	$\dfrac{5}{10}$
0.07	$\dfrac{7}{10}$

Name _____

Dollars and Cents

 Directions: Look at the groups of coins in each box. Write the symbol for more than (>), less than (<), or equal to (=) on the line.

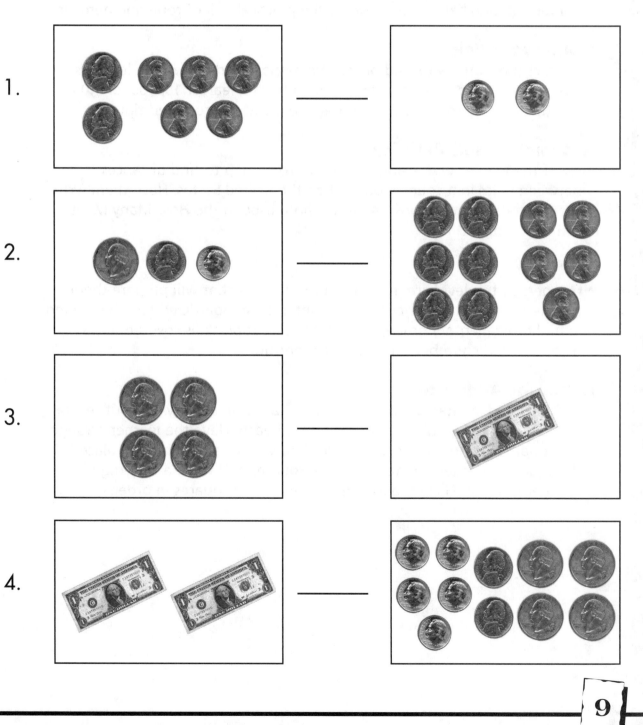

1. _____

2. _____

3. _____

4. _____

9

Background
• This section enhances learners' understanding of place value and large numbers. It also helps them develop the practical skill of rounding numbers.

Homework Helper
• Instruct the learners to find prices in newspaper ads. Have the learners write down the prices, then round them to the nearest 10, 100, or 1,000. Ask the learners to explain how they arrived at the rounded figures.

Research-based Activity
• Assist the learner with using an atlas or road map to find distances between cities in a country other than the United States. Have them write the distances as equations similar to those used in the How Many Miles? activity on page 11.

Test Prep
• Learners at this level are introduced to activities that will prepare them for the testing format they will encounter on standardized tests beginning in higher elementary grades. The test-preparation skills covered in this section include number sense and sequencing.

Different Audiences
• A challenged learner will benefit from a hands-on activity. Cut out several squares and write a three-digit number on each. Have the learner arrange the squares in numerical order. Once the learner has successfully placed the squares in order, create additional squares and write a four-digit number on each. Have the learner arrange these squares in order.

TEACHING TIPS

10

Name _____

How Many Miles?

0, 1, 2, 3, 4, 5, 6, 7, 8, or 9 are digits used to write numbers. The place value of a digit gives the value of that digit as it appears in a number. *Example:* 1,423 = 1 thousand + 4 hundreds + 2 tens + 3 ones

 Directions: Write the numbers that show how many miles there are between the following cities.

1. New York City, New York, to Mackinaw City, Michigan
   9 hundreds + 1 ten + 4 ones = _____ miles

2. Mackinaw City, Michigan, to Indianapolis, Indiana
   4 hundreds + 8 tens + 9 ones = _____ miles

3. Indianapolis, Indiana, to Duluth, Minnesota
   7 hundreds + 5 tens + 4 ones = _____ miles

4. Duluth, Minnesota, to Spokane, Washington
   1 thousand + 4 hundreds + 2 tens + 3 ones = _____ miles

5. Spokane, Washington, to San Francisco, California
   1 thousand + 0 hundreds + 3 tens + 7 ones = _____ miles

FUN FACT

The distance from New York City, New York, to San Francisco, California, is 2,945 miles.

11

Name _____

Put Them in Order

Numbers can be placed in order of their value. The order can be from highest to lowest numbers or from lowest to highest numbers.
Example: The following numbers are in order from lowest to highest:
560, 672, 780, 825, 900.

 Directions: Arrange the following penny collections in order, from lowest to highest, by numbering them from 1 to 8 on the lines in the pigs.

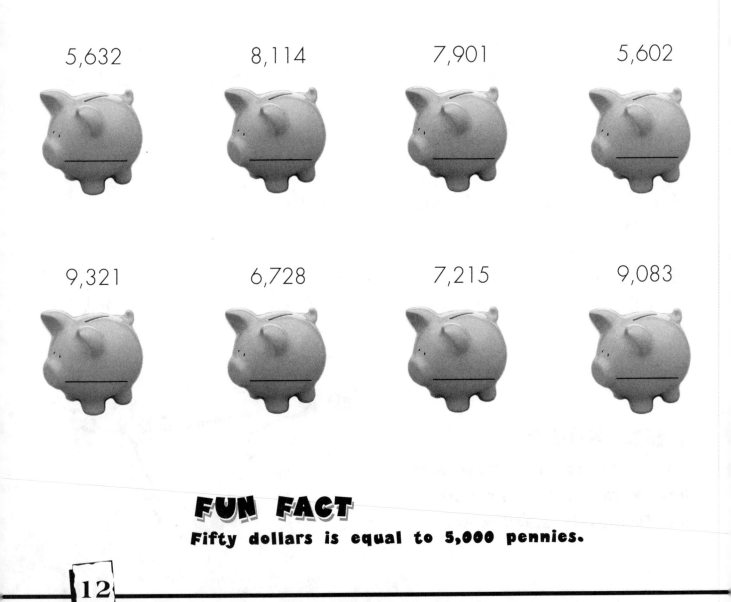

5,632   8,114   7,901   5,602

9,321   6,728   7,215   9,083

FUN FACT
Fifty dollars is equal to 5,000 pennies.

Name _____

Tens and Hundreds

To round to *the nearest 10*, round up if the number in the ones place is 5 or greater. Round down if the number in the ones place is 4 or less.
Example: The number 23 rounded to the nearest 10 is 20 since 3 is less than 5.
To round to *the nearest 100*, round up if the number in the tens place is 5 or greater. Round down if the number in the tens place is 4 or less.
Example: The number 172 rounded to the nearest 100 is 200 since 7 is greater than 5.

Directions: Below are the amounts of fruits and vegetables sold at Country Farm Store in a week. Round each number below, then write the rounded number on the line.

Round to the nearest 10	Round to the nearest 100
1. 72 kiwis _____	6. 114 beets _____
2. 56 plums _____	7. 429 carrots _____
3. 37 avocados _____	8. 190 tomatoes _____
4. 81 pears _____	9. 552 apples _____
5. 25 watermelons _____	10. 275 oranges _____

FUN FACT

In a single acre of rain forest, you might find 294 different kinds of trees. That's about 300 kinds of trees.

Name _____

Rounding Up or Down

To round to *the nearest 100*, round up if the number in the tens place is 5 or greater. Round down if the number in the tens place is 4 or less.
Example: The number 172 rounded to the nearest 100 is 200 since 7 is greater than 5.
To round to *the nearest 1,000*, round up if the number in the hundreds place is 5 or greater. Round down if the number in the hundreds place is 4 or less.
Example: The number 3,540 rounded to the nearest 1,000 is 4,000 since the number in the hundreds place is 5.

 Directions: Round the numbers to the nearest hundred and thousand, and write the rounded numbers on the lines.

Round to the nearest 100

1. 795 _____

2. 627 _____

3. 188 _____

4. 909 _____

5. 536 _____

Round to the nearest 1,000

6. 4,830 _____

7. 1,219 _____

8. 8,144 _____

9. 5,450 _____

10. 6,749 _____

FUN FACT

Orcas, or killer whales, can weigh 10,255 pounds (4,652 kilograms). An average orca can eat 3,857 pounds (1,750 kg) of food in 1 week!

14

Name _____

Skill Check—Whole Numbers

Ordering Numbers

 Directions: Here are the populations for towns in Alaska in 2000. On a separate sheet of paper, list the numbers in order from lowest to highest.

Barrow	4,581	Nome	3,505
Kenai	6,942	Seward	2,635
Ketchikan	7,922	Sitka	8,835
Kodiak	6,334	Valdez	4,036

Rounding Numbers

Directions: Round the following numbers to the nearest hundred or thousand. Write the rounded numbers on the lines.

Round to the nearest 100   Round to the nearest 1,000

1. 795 _____   6. 2,395 _____

2. 104 _____   7. 3,208 _____

3. 811 _____   8. 10,600 _____

4. 652 _____   9. 8,903 _____

5. 629 _____   10. 1,300 _____

15

© Rosen School Supply•Brain Builders Numbers and Operations•3•RSS-8572-5

Teaching Tips...

Background
• Learners strengthen their addition and subtraction skills by solving
number and word problems involving two-, three-, and four-digit numbers.

Homework Helper
• Provide extra practice for learners by creating word problems that are
based on the learners' lives. For example, use the distance traveled to
school or number of items bought while grocery shopping in the problems.

Research-based Activity
• Ask learners to find newspaper or magazine articles containing three- and
four-digit numbers. Assist the learners with creating their own
word problems based on the articles. Then have them solve the problems.

Test Prep
• These activities will prepare learners for standardized tests. The test-
preparation skills covered in this section include computational skills
and solving word problems.

Different Audiences
• Show an accelerated learner how to perform addition and subtraction
using an abacus. Give him or her several problems to solve. For an
additional challenge, time the learner as he or she solves each problem.

TEACHING TIPS

Name _____

Number Problems

To add two numbers is to join them together to find a sum, or total amount.

Example:
$$\begin{array}{r} 420 \\ +35 \\ \hline 455 \end{array}$$

Directions: Solve the following problems with addition. Use a separate sheet of paper if you need more space.

1. $\begin{array}{r} 35 \\ +\ 56 \\ \hline \end{array}$ 2. $\begin{array}{r} 57 \\ +\ 52 \\ \hline \end{array}$ 3. $\begin{array}{r} 63 \\ +48 \\ \hline \end{array}$ 4. $\begin{array}{r} 79 \\ +61 \\ \hline \end{array}$

5. $\begin{array}{r} 162 \\ +\ 39 \\ \hline \end{array}$ 6. $\begin{array}{r} 273 \\ +54 \\ \hline \end{array}$ 7. $\begin{array}{r} 306 \\ +\ 207 \\ \hline \end{array}$ 8. $\begin{array}{r} 294 \\ +\ 258 \\ \hline \end{array}$

9. $\begin{array}{r} 3,932 \\ +\ 2,584 \\ \hline \end{array}$ 10. $\begin{array}{r} 8,579 \\ +\ 2,962 \\ \hline \end{array}$ 11. $\begin{array}{r} 5,985 \\ +\ 6,375 \\ \hline \end{array}$ 12. $\begin{array}{r} 7,036 \\ +\ 4,987 \\ \hline \end{array}$

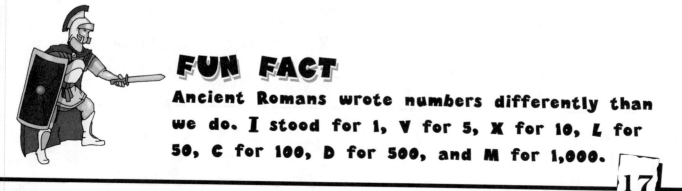

FUN FACT

Ancient Romans wrote numbers differently than we do. I stood for 1, V for 5, X for 10, L for 50, C for 100, D for 500, and M for 1,000.

17

Name _____

Word Problems

Read word problems carefully to understand what you need to add.
Then find the numbers and add them together.
Example: Yesterday at Mr. Jones's hardware store, customers bought
25 lightbulbs. Today Mr. Jones sold 60 more lightbulbs. How
many lightbulbs did Mr. Jones sell? 60 + 25 = 85 lightbulbs

Directions: Use addition to solve the following word problems. Use a separate sheet of paper to work out your answers.

1. Ray traveled 156 miles from Peach Town to Park Village. Then he traveled 134 miles from Park Village to Watertown. How many miles did Joe travel altogether? _____

2. Diane and Lisa like to read books. In June they borrowed 12 books from the library. In July they borrowed 10. How many books did Diane and Lisa borrow in the 2 months? _____

3. Mr. Smith and Ms. Jones are taking their third-grade students on a field trip to the museum. Mr. Smith is taking 75 students and Ms. Jones is taking 50 students. How many students will there be on the field trip? _____

4. The Very Loud Music Store sold 2,500 music compact discs last month. This month the store sold 1,000 compact discs. How many music compact discs did the store sell in the past two months?

_____

18

Name _____

Number Problems

To subtract one number from another, take the smaller number from the larger number.

Example:
$$\begin{array}{r} 90 \\ -76 \\ \hline 14 \end{array}$$

Directions: Solve the following subtraction problems. Use a separate sheet of paper if you need more space.

1.
$$\begin{array}{r} 20 \\ -19 \\ \hline \end{array}$$

2.
$$\begin{array}{r} 89 \\ -37 \\ \hline \end{array}$$

3.
$$\begin{array}{r} 43 \\ -27 \\ \hline \end{array}$$

4.
$$\begin{array}{r} 78 \\ -52 \\ \hline \end{array}$$

5.
$$\begin{array}{r} 177 \\ -95 \\ \hline \end{array}$$

6.
$$\begin{array}{r} 624 \\ -232 \\ \hline \end{array}$$

7.
$$\begin{array}{r} 256 \\ -152 \\ \hline \end{array}$$

8.
$$\begin{array}{r} 983 \\ -354 \\ \hline \end{array}$$

9.
$$\begin{array}{r} 5,201 \\ -4,211 \\ \hline \end{array}$$

10.
$$\begin{array}{r} 8,309 \\ -5,107 \\ \hline \end{array}$$

11.
$$\begin{array}{r} 2,744 \\ -2,621 \\ \hline \end{array}$$

12.
$$\begin{array}{r} 6,580 \\ -3,479 \\ \hline \end{array}$$

FUN FACT

There are two types of deserts: hot, dry deserts and cold deserts.

Name _____

Word Problems

Read word problems carefully to understand what you need to subtract.
Then find the numbers and subtract them from each other.
Example: Alice had 10 pencils. She gave 5 pencils to Jane. How many
pencils did she have left?   10 – 5 = 5 pencils

 **Directions: Solve the following word problems using
subtraction. Use a separate sheet of paper to work
out your answers.**

1. Greg picked 145 strawberries. Kerri picked 258 strawberries. How
many more strawberries did Kerri pick?

   _____

2. Jane and her brother picked 315 blueberries. Paul and his sister picked
532 blueberries. How many more blueberries did Paul and his sister pick?

   _____

3. Mary Ann's family picked 850 gooseberries and 700 blackberries.
How many more gooseberries did Mary Ann's family pick?

   _____

4. Colleen picked 24 green apples and 35 red apples. How many
more red apples did Colleen pick?

   _____

5. Chris picked 15 peaches. Jen picked 12 peaches. How many more
peaches did Chris pick?

   _____

FUN FACT
There are about 600 different kinds of strawberries.

Name _____

Skill Check—Addition and Subtraction

👉 **Directions: Solve the following word problems with subtraction and addition. Use a separate sheet of paper to work out your answers.**

1. The Hawaiian island of Maui covers 728 square miles. The Hawaiian island of Oahu covers 594 square miles. How many square miles do the 2 islands cover altogether?

_____

2. About 2,965 people live on the Hawaiian island of Lanai. About 7,275 people live on the Hawaiian island of Molokai. About how many people live on the 2 islands altogether?

_____

3. There used to be about 72 kinds of birds that were found only in Hawaii. About 39 of those kinds of birds no longer exist. How many of these birds are left in Hawaii?

_____

4. The highest temperature ever recorded in Hawaii was 100 degrees. The lowest temperature ever recorded was 12 degrees. How much warmer was the highest temperature?

_____

Teaching Tips...

Background

• In this section, learners strengthen their multiplication and division skills by solving number and word problems.

Homework Helper

• Have the learner complete a multiplication table. Draw a grid with nine columns and nine rows. Write the numbers 1 through 9 above the columns and to the left of the rows. Have the learner fill in each box with the product of the number found above the column and the number to the left of the row. (Examples: The number 1 goes in the first box of the first row, since 1 x 1 = 1. The number 6 goes in the third box of the second row, since 2 x 3 = 6.)

Research-based Activity

• Assist the learner in using a software program that gives them practice solving division problems and helps them understand the inverse relationship between multiplication and division.

Test Prep

• Learners at this level are introduced to activities that will prepare them for the testing format they will encounter on standardized tests beginning in higher elementary grades. The test-preparation skills covered in this section include computational skills and solving word problems.

Different Audiences

• Prepare a set of flash cards for an English as a second language (ESL) learner. On one side, write multiplication and division vocabulary words in English (*factor, product, multiplier, dividend, divisor, quotient,* etc.). On the other side, write the terms in the learner's native language. Use the flash cards for vocabulary reinforcement.

© Rosen School Supply•Brain Builders Numbers and Operations•3•RSS-8572-5

Name _____

Number Problems

Multiplication is a short way to add the same number a certain number of times.

Example: 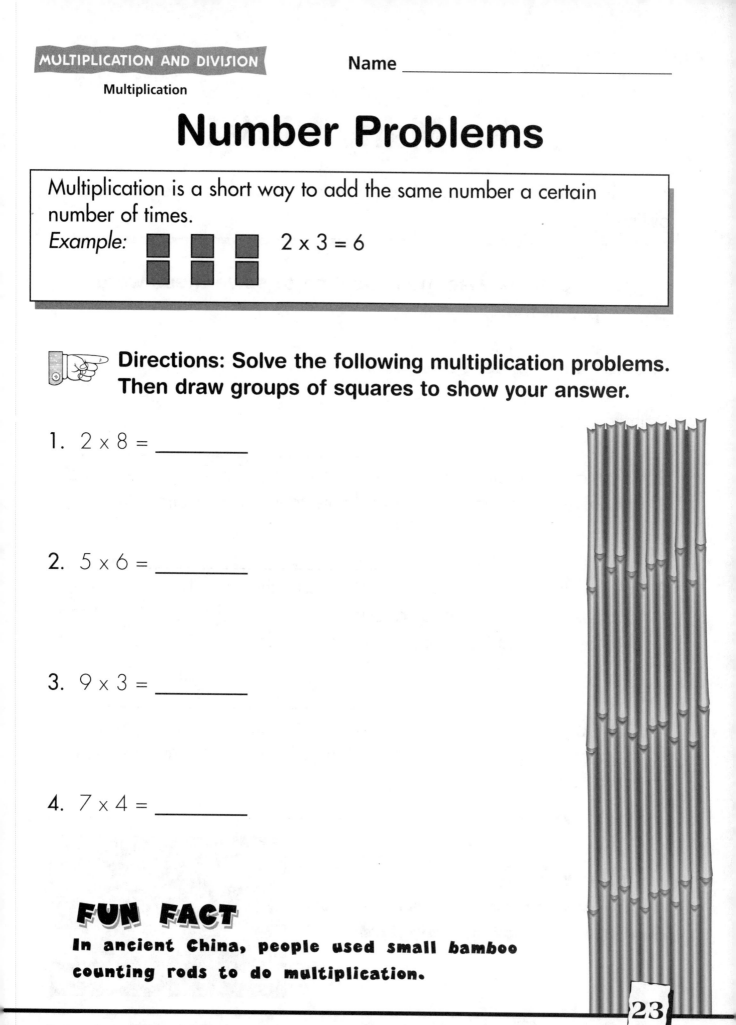 2 x 3 = 6

Directions: Solve the following multiplication problems. Then draw groups of squares to show your answer.

1. 2 x 8 = _____

2. 5 x 6 = _____

3. 9 x 3 = _____

4. 7 x 4 = _____

FUN FACT

In ancient China, people used small bamboo counting rods to do multiplication.

23

Name _____

So Many Birds!

Multiplication is a short way to add the same number a certain number of times.

 Directions: Use multiplication to solve these word problems.

1. Barbara had 5 feeders full of sugar water for hummingbirds. There are 3 hummingbirds at each feeder. How many hummingbirds are there altogether?

_____

2. Barbara had 2 birdbaths for the birds to bathe in. There are 9 birds at each birdbath. How many birds are there at both birdbaths?

_____

3. Barbara has 4 feeders shaped like houses that are filled with seed for birds. There are 8 birds at each house-shaped feeder. How many birds are there at the house-shaped feeders?

_____

4. Barbara has 3 trays of peanuts for woodpeckers and blue jays. There are 11 birds at each peanut tray. How many birds are there at the peanut trays?

_____

There are 214 kinds of woodpeckers and 328 kinds of hummingbirds.

Name _____

Number Problems

To find out how many times a number can be divided by another, divide the larger number by the smaller.

Example:

$$\overset{3}{3\overline{)9}}$$

👉 **Directions: On a separate sheet of paper, solve the following division problems.**

1.

$$2\overline{)8}$$

2.

$$3\overline{)30}$$

3.

$$2\overline{)34}$$

4.

$$5\overline{)55}$$

5.

$$3\overline{)48}$$

6.

$$5\overline{)95}$$

7.

$$5\overline{)75}$$

8.

$$3\overline{)42}$$

9.

$$7\overline{)91}$$

FUN FACT

The answer to a division problem is called the quotient. This name comes from a Latin word that means "how many times."

Name _____

Remainders

To find out how many times a number can be divided by another, divide the larger number by the smaller. Sometimes a number cannot be divided equally into another number. The amount that is left over is called the remainder.

Example:

$$\frac{4}{2\overline{)9}}$$ Remainder = 1

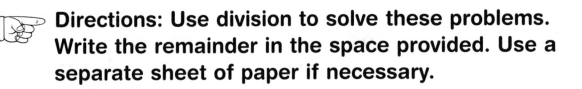

Directions: Use division to solve these problems. Write the remainder in the space provided. Use a separate sheet of paper if necessary.

1.
$$7\overline{)15}$$

Remainder = ____

2.
$$3\overline{)10}$$

Remainder = ____

3.
$$5\overline{)33}$$

Remainder = ____

4.
$$4\overline{)20}$$

Remainder = ____

5.
$$6\overline{)38}$$

Remainder = ____

6.
$$2\overline{)27}$$

Remainder = ____

FUN FACT

In a division problem, the number that is divided is called the dividend. This name comes from a Latin word that means "to separate."

26

Name _____

Skill Check—Multiplication and Division

Number Problems

 Directions: Solve the number problems using multiplication and division. Use a separate sheet of paper if necessary.

1. 21
   x 5

2. 13
   x 6

3. 78
   x 3

4. 54
   x 7

5. 36
   x 4

6. 4⟌84

7. 3⟌45

8. 2⟌28

9. 4⟌38

10. 3⟌75

Word Problems

Directions: Solve the word problems using multiplication.

1. Nancy, Dave, Joan, and Diane checked out books from the library. Each of them checked out 6 books. How many books did they check out altogether?

   _____

2. Gary, Mike, Pam, Cindy, and Connie helped the library van take books to people at home. Each of them handed out 13 books. How many books did they hand out altogether?

   _____

© Rosen School Supply•Brain Builders Numbers and Operations•3•RSS-8572-5

Background
• The activities in this section give learners practice in adding and subtracting fractions and mixed numbers. For example, the activity on page 32 allows learners to practice translating percentages to fractions.

Homework Helper
• Have learners practice applying fractions to daily life. Ask them to divide fixed quantities of food into a prescribed number of equal units. For example, cut a pan of brownies into twelfths or a pizza into eighths.

Research-based Activity
• Work together with the learner to find a simple recipe that contains fractions and mixed numbers on the Internet. Prepare the recipe with the learner. Then have the learner write the amount of each ingredient they would need if they doubled the recipe.

Test Prep
• These activities prepare learners for the testing format they will encounter on standardized tests beginning in higher elementary grades. The test-preparation skills covered in this section include computational skills and following written directions.

Different Audiences
• Assist an accelerated learner in gathering information about their town or city from the U.S. Census Bureau Web site. Have them record percentages such as the percent of the population who live in cities or the percent who have graduated from college. Then work together with the learner to create and solve addition and subtraction problems using these percentages.

Name _____

Finding Fractions

The top number of a fraction is called the numerator. The bottom number is called the denominator. $\dfrac{1}{2}$ ← numerator
← denominator

Add or subtract the numerators. The denominator stays the same.

Example: $\dfrac{1}{3} + \dfrac{1}{3} = \dfrac{2}{3}$

Directions: Add or subtract the fractions. Then color in the fraction of the box that represents your answer.

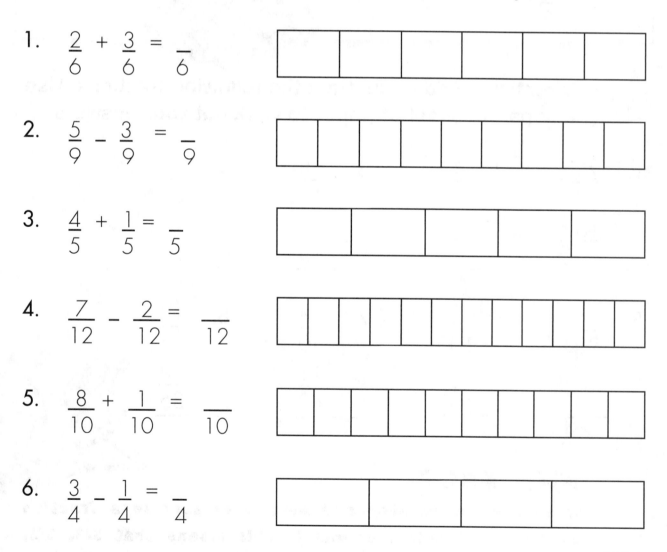

1. $\dfrac{2}{6} + \dfrac{3}{6} = \dfrac{}{6}$

2. $\dfrac{5}{9} - \dfrac{3}{9} = \dfrac{}{9}$

3. $\dfrac{4}{5} + \dfrac{1}{5} = \dfrac{}{5}$

4. $\dfrac{7}{12} - \dfrac{2}{12} = \dfrac{}{12}$

5. $\dfrac{8}{10} + \dfrac{1}{10} = \dfrac{}{10}$

6. $\dfrac{3}{4} - \dfrac{1}{4} = \dfrac{}{4}$

Name _____

Plus or Minus

The top number of a fraction is called the numerator. The bottom number is called the denominator. $\dfrac{1}{2}$ ← numerator
← denominator

Add or subtract the numerators. The denominator stays the same.

Example:

$$\dfrac{1}{3} + \dfrac{1}{3} = \dfrac{2}{3}$$

 Directions: Add or subtract the following fractions. Use a separate sheet of paper to work out your answers.

1. $\dfrac{25}{50}$
    $+\dfrac{10}{50}$

2. $\dfrac{12}{22}$
    $-\dfrac{9}{22}$

3. $\dfrac{8}{15}$
    $+\dfrac{7}{15}$

4. $\dfrac{50}{80}$
    $-\dfrac{11}{80}$

5. $\dfrac{16}{20}$
    $+\dfrac{5}{20}$

6. $\dfrac{60}{100}$
    $-\dfrac{6}{100}$

7. $\dfrac{24}{40}$
    $+\dfrac{11}{40}$

8. $\dfrac{10}{35}$
    $-\dfrac{8}{35}$

FUN FACT

When the top number and bottom number in a fraction match, the fraction equals 1. This means that 3/3, 5/5, 10/10, and 13/13 all equal 1.

30

Name _____

How Much Do You Need?

A number made up of a whole number and a fraction is called a mixed number. To add or subtract mixed numbers, add or subtract the fractions first. Then add or subtract the whole numbers. *Example:*

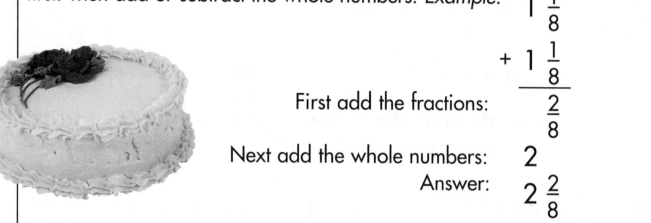

$$1 \frac{1}{8}$$
$$+ 1 \frac{1}{8}$$

First add the fractions: $\frac{2}{8}$

Next add the whole numbers: 2

Answer: $2 \frac{2}{8}$

 Directions: Add or subtract the problems below.

1. A cake recipe calls for 1 and 1/4 cups of sugar and 2 and 1/4 cups of flour. How many cups of sugar and flour combined does the cake need?

$$2 \frac{1}{4}$$
$$+ 1 \frac{1}{4}$$

_____ cups of flour

2. Ray rode his bicycle for 5 and 1/5 miles on Tuesday. On Wednesday, he rode for 4 and 2/5 miles. How many miles did Ray ride altogether?

$$5 \frac{1}{5}$$
$$+ 4 \frac{2}{5}$$

_____ miles

Name _____

America's People

A percentage is a fraction written as parts out of 100. The symbol % means percent. To write a percent as a fraction, show the percent number over 100.

Example: $7\% = \dfrac{7}{100}$

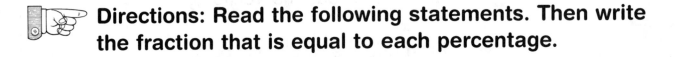 **Directions: Read the following statements. Then write the fraction that is equal to each percentage.**

1. In the United States, 14% of the people are from 15 years old to 24 years old. $14\% = \dfrac{}{100}$

2. Of the people who now live in the United States, 11% were born in other countries. $11\% = \dfrac{}{100}$

3. Out of every 100 people in the United States, 18 speak a language besides English at home. $18\% = \dfrac{}{100}$

4. In the United States, 80% of the people have graduated from high school. $80\% = \dfrac{}{100}$

5. Out of every 100 people in the United States, 24 have graduated from college. $24\% = \dfrac{}{100}$

FUN FACT
The percent symbol % was invented around 1500. It was first used in business records.

32

Name _____

Skill Check—Fractions

Mixed Numbers

👉 **Directions: Solve the following mixed number problems by adding or subtracting.**

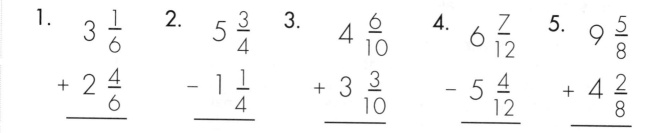

1. $3\frac{1}{6}$
    $+ 2\frac{4}{6}$

2. $5\frac{3}{4}$
    $- 1\frac{1}{4}$

3. $4\frac{6}{10}$
    $+ 3\frac{3}{10}$

4. $6\frac{7}{12}$
    $- 5\frac{4}{12}$

5. $9\frac{5}{8}$
    $+ 4\frac{2}{8}$

Percentages

👉 **Directions: Write the fraction that is equal to each percentage.**

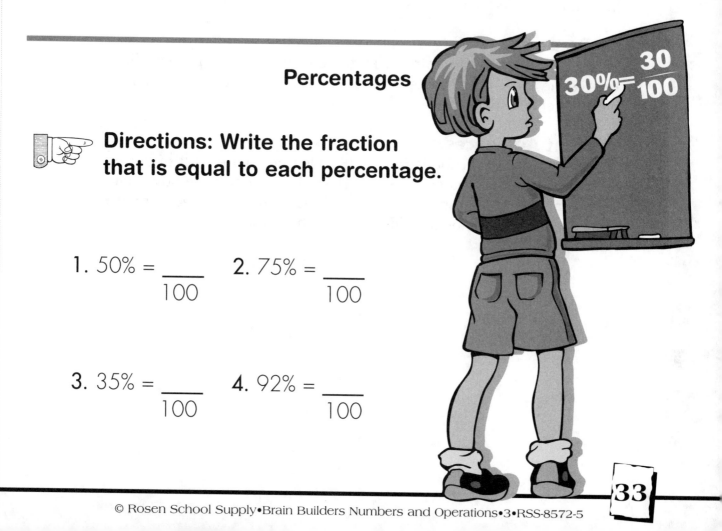

$30\% = \frac{30}{100}$

1. $50\% = \dfrac{}{100}$ 2. $75\% = \dfrac{}{100}$

3. $35\% = \dfrac{}{100}$ 4. $92\% = \dfrac{}{100}$

33

Teaching Tips...

Background
• The activities in this section introduce decimals as another way to write fractions and mixed numbers. Learners also practice adding and subtracting decimals.

Homework Helper
• Help learners to practice reading decimals. Write out in words several decimals. For example, two-tenths or one and seven-tenths. Have the learner write each decimal using numbers and a decimal point.

Research-based Activity
• Ask learners to use the Internet to find who the first people were to introduce the first decimal system.

Test Prep
• Learners at this level are introduced to activities that will prepare them for the testing format they will encounter on standardized tests beginning in higher elementary grades.

Different Audiences
• For an English as a second language (ESL) learner, write a list of decimals, including decimals greater than one. Have the learner write how they would say the number in their native language. Assist the learner with pronouncing the numbers in English. Then have them write the numbers in English.

TEACHING TIPS

34

Name _____

Matching the Fraction

A decimal is a number that includes a decimal point and one or two numbers to the right of the decimal point. The numbers to the left of the decimal point are whole numbers. The numbers to the right of the point are fractions.

Example: $2.1 = 2\frac{1}{10}$

Directions: Draw a line from each decimal to its matching fraction.

.2 $\frac{6}{10}$

5.8 $7\frac{9}{10}$

.6 $6\frac{4}{10}$

9.1 $\frac{3}{10}$

.5 $\frac{2}{10}$

6.4 $9\frac{1}{10}$

.3 $5\frac{8}{10}$

7.9 $\frac{5}{10}$

Name _____

Adding and Subtracting Decimals

To add or subtract decimal numbers, line up the decimal points of the numbers. Next add or subtract the numbers. Then move the decimal point down into your answer.

Example:

```
   .3          .7
 + .2        - .5
 ↓           ↓
  .5          .2
```

Directions: Add or subtract to solve the problems. Remember to carry the decimal point down into your answer.

```
1.   .1      2.   .8      3.   .4      4.   .9      5.   .5
   + .4        - .3        + .3        - .3        + .1


6.   .8      7.   .6      8.   .4      9.   .5      10.  .8
   + .4        - .5        + .2        - .2         + .1
```

FUN FACT

The decimal point was invented in Holland around 1610.

Name _____

Decimals Greater Than 1

Decimals greater than 1 can be written as mixed number fractions.
Example: $3.2 = 3\frac{2}{10}$

Directions: Write each mixed number as a decimal.

1. $1\frac{7}{10}$ _____

2. $5\frac{3}{10}$ _____

3. $2\frac{9}{10}$ _____

4. $8\frac{1}{10}$ _____

5. $4\frac{6}{10}$ _____

6. $9\frac{9}{10}$ _____

7. $3\frac{4}{10}$ _____

8. $7\frac{8}{10}$ _____

9. $2\frac{5}{10}$ _____

10. $8\frac{2}{10}$ _____

FUN FACT

The word "decimal" comes from the Latin word "decimus," which means "tenth."

Name _____

Adding and Subtracting Decimals Greater Than 1

Decimals greater than 1 are added and subtracted just like whole numbers. To add or subtract decimal numbers, line up the decimal points of the numbers. Next add or subtract the numbers. Then move the decimal point down into your answer.

Example:

$$2.3 + 4.1 = 6.4$$

$$6.9 - 3.6 = 3.3$$

👉 **Directions: Add or subtract to solve the problems. Remember to carry the decimal point down into your answer.**

1. $4.5 + 3.3$ 2. $7.8 - 4.6$ 3. $3.7 + 5.2$ 4. $9.8 - 7.7$ 5. $5.4 + 4.3$

6. $2.7 + 5.4$ 7. $6.5 - 3.8$ 8. $4.3 + 3.9$ 9. $9.1 - 7.2$ 10. $5.5 + 2.6$

FUN FACT

When we buy gas for our cars, parts of a gallon are given in decimals. For example, 8.7 gallons equals $8\frac{7}{10}$ gallons.

38

Name _____

Skill Check—Decimals

Decimals and Mixed Numbers

👉 **Directions: Write each fraction or mixed number as a decimal.**

1. $1\frac{7}{10}$ _____

2. $\frac{5}{10}$ _____

3. $\frac{3}{10}$ _____

4. $6\frac{2}{10}$ _____

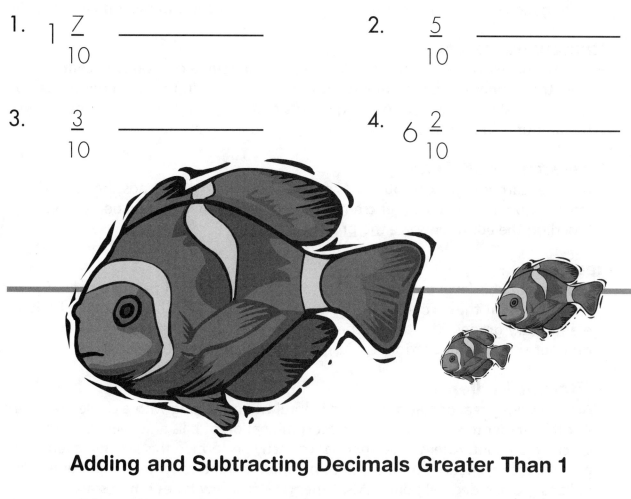

Adding and Subtracting Decimals Greater Than 1

👉 **Directions: Add or subtract to solve the problems.**

1. 5.7
    $+ 3.1$

2. 7.5
    $- 4.3$

3. 2.8
    $+ 2.6$

4. 9.3
    $- 7.6$

5. 5.7
    $+ 3.4$

Teaching Tips...

Background

• The activities in this section give learners practice in recognizing money values and writing money amounts. Learners also solve addition and subtraction word problems.

Homework Helper

• Extend the activities on page 41. Write several amounts of money in cents. Then have the learner write the amounts using dollar signs and decimal points. Say or write several money amounts using dollars and cents, and ask the learner to write the amounts in numbers, using dollar signs and decimals points.

Research-based Activity

• Ask the learner to look through newspapers for grocery store ads that contain price information. Have the learner create several addition and subtraction problems based on the ads, then solve the problems.

Test Prep

• Learners at this level are introduced to activities that will prepare them for the testing format they will encounter on standardized tests beginning in higher elementary grades. The test-preparation skills covered in this section include number sense, computational skills, and solving word problems.

Different Audiences

• Activities using real or play money are helpful when working with a challenged learner. Ask the learner to show you the correct combination of bills and coins to match a specified amount. After the learner has correctly performed this activity several times, give them combinations of bills and coins, and ask them to write the amounts using dollar signs and decimal points. Assist them the first few times if necessary.

Name _____

Using Decimals to Write Money Amounts

When showing an amount of money, we use the dollar sign ($) to show the dollar amount. We use the cent sign (¢) to show the cent amount. A decimal point is placed after the dollar amount and before the cent amount. *Example:* 5 dollars = $5.00

25 cents = 0.25¢

To show a dollar amount as well as a cent amount, use only the dollar sign and the decimal point. *Example:* 2 dollars and 6 cents = $2.06

 Directions: Circle the correct answer that shows the dollars and cents amounts for each question below.

1. 8 dollars and 65 cents =
   A. $8.065   B. $ .865
   C. $86.50   D. $8.65

2. 6 dollars and 8 cents =
   A. $6.80   B. 0.68¢
   C. $6.08   D. $68.00

3. 12 dollars and 20 cents =
   A. $12.20   B. $122.00
   C. $1.22   D. $12.02

4. 73 cents =
   A. $1.73   B. $17.03
   C. 0.73¢   D. $17.30

5. 20 dollars and 6 cents =
   A. $20.60   B. $26.00
   C. $2.06   D. $20.06

FUN FACT

A penny is $\frac{1}{100}$ of a dollar, or .01 dollar. A dime is $\frac{1}{10}$ of a dollar, or .10 dollar.

41

Name _____

Greater Than, Less Than, or Equal To?

By learning the value of coins and paper money, we can tell how much they are worth.

Example: ⬤⬤⬤⬤⬤ < ⬤⬤⬤

 Directions: Compare the value of the sums of money below. Then in the space provided, write the symbol for more than (>), less than (<), or equal to (=).

1.	____	
2.	____	
3.	____	
4.	____	

FUN FACT

Another name for a penny is a "cent." "Cent" comes from a Latin word that means "hundred."

Name _____

Shopping at the Farmers' Market

We can add amounts of money the same way we add decimals.

 Directions: Use a separate sheet of paper to solve the following problems.

1. At the farmers' market, Jason spent $1.30 on yellow squash and $2.15 on green squash. How much did he spend on squash altogether?

   _____

2. Jenny spent $3.25 on corn and $2.60 on green beans at the farmers' market. How much did she spend on vegetables altogether?

   _____

3. Valerie spent $5.43 on strawberries and $4.52 on blueberries at the farmers' market. How much did she spend on berries altogether?

   _____

4. Ralph spent $6.80 on red apples and $7.35 on green apples at the farmers' market. How much did he spend on apples altogether?

   _____

5. Rachel spent $5.69 on 3 loaves of white bread and $8.52 on 4 loaves of whole wheat bread at the farmers' market. How much did she spend on bread altogether?

   _____

6. Paul spent $14.24 on peach pies and $12.98 on apple pies at the farmers' market. How much did he spend on pies altogether?

   _____

FUN FACT

At a farmers' market, you can buy fruit and vegetables from the farmers who grew them. You can also buy homemade jellies, jams, pies, and breads.

43

Name _____

Shopping at the Bookstore

We can subtract amounts of money just like we subtract decimals.

👉 **Directions: Use a separate sheet of paper to solve the following problems.**

1. Becky and her friends went to the bookstore to buy some books. Becky had $15.00 to spend. She bought a book about a family who traveled west on a wagon train. The book cost $10.00. How much money did Becky have left? _____

2. Kevin bought a book about dinosaurs. He had $12.75 to spend. The book cost $11.50. How much money did Kevin have left?

_____

3. Lisa bought a book about hummingbirds. She had $9.83 to spend. The book cost $7.12. How much money did Lisa have left?

_____

4. Dylan bought a book about Renaissance art. He had $25.50 to spend. The book cost $14.95. How much money did Dylan have left?

_____

5. Peter bought a book about stamp collecting. He had $17.23 to spend. The book cost $9.88. How much money did Peter have left?

_____

FUN FACT

The United States dollar takes its name from an old type of German coin called a taler.

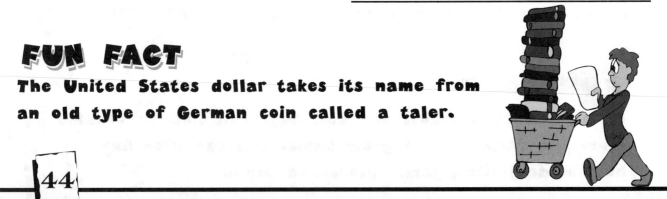

44

Name _____

Skill Check—Money

Adding and Subtracting Money

Directions: Use addition to solve the problems. Use a separate sheet of paper, if necessary.

1. Sue took her brother Max to the ice cream shop and bought ice cream for both of them. Her ice cream cone cost $1.15. Max got a larger dish of ice cream for $1.70. How much did Sue spend on ice cream altogether? _____

2. Peggy and her twin sister Pam bought new sunglasses. Peggy spent $7.73 for her sunglasses. Pam spent $8.22 for her sunglasses. How much did Peggy and Pam spend altogether?

   _____

3. Larry and Dan bought books about trains. Larry spent $15.67 for his book. Dan spent $17.55 for his book. How much did Larry and Dan spend altogether? _____

4. Maggie had $9.65. She spent $6.40 to buy a new fish for her fish tank. How much money did Maggie have left?

   _____

5. Erik had $8.57. He spent $7.74 on flowers for his garden. How much money did Erik have left? _____

6. Kate had $12.34. She spent $10.87 on a gift for her father. How much money did Kate have left? _____

© Rosen School Supply•Brain Builders Numbers and Operations•3•RSS-8572-5

Answer Key

p. 4
1. 537 books
2. 975 books
3. 7930 books
4. 1355 books
5. 190 books

p. 5
1. 103 hamburgers and hot dogs
2. 171 stamps
3. 66 flowers
4. 344 houses

p. 6
1. 85
2. 18
3. 180
4. 112
5. 125
6. 56
7. 64
8. 48
9. 30

p. 7
1. 3/4

2. 7/9

3. 1/5

4. 4/8

p. 8

0.7 — $\frac{2}{10}$

0.8 — $\frac{7}{100}$

0.5 — $\frac{3}{100}$

0.03 — $\frac{8}{10}$

0.2 — $\frac{5}{10}$

0.07 — $\frac{7}{10}$

p. 9
1. <
2. >
3. =
4. >

p. 11
1. 914 miles
2. 489 miles
3. 754 miles
4. 1,423 miles
5. 1,037 miles

p. 12
1. 5,602
2. 5,632
3. 6,728
4. 7,215
5. 7,901
6. 8,114
7. 9,083
8. 9,321

p. 13
1. 70
2. 60
3. 40
4. 80
5. 30
6. 100
7. 400
8. 200
9. 600
10. 300

p. 14
1. 800
2. 600
3. 200
4. 900
5. 500
6. 5,000
7. 1,000
8. 8,000
9. 5,000
10. 7,000

p. 15
Ordering Numbers

Seward	2,635
Nome	3,505
Valdez	4,036
Barrow	4,581
Kodiak	6,334
Kenai	6,942
Ketchikan	7,922
Sitka	8,835

Rounding Numbers
1. 800
2. 100
3. 800
4. 700
5. 600
6. 2,000
7. 3,000
8. 11,000
9. 9,000
10. 1,000

p. 17
1. 91
2. 109
3. 111
4. 140
5. 201
6. 327
7. 513
8. 552

9. 6,516 11. 12,360
10. 11,541 12. 12,023

p. 18
1. 290 miles
2. 22 books
3. 125 students
4. 3,500 compact discs

p. 19
1. 1 7. 104
2. 52 8. 629
3. 16 9. 990
4. 26 10. 3,202
5. 82 11. 123
6. 392 12. 3,101

p. 20
1. 113 more strawberries
2. 217 more blueberries
3. 150 more gooseberries
4. 11 more red apples
5. 3 more peaches

p. 21
1. 1,322 square miles
2. 10,240 people
3. 33 kinds of birds
4. 88 degrees

p. 23
1. 16
2. 30
3. 27
4. 28

p. 24
1. 15 hummingbirds
2. 18 birds
3. 32 birds
4. 33 woodpeckers and blue jays

p. 25
1. 4 6. 19
2. 10 7. 15
3. 17 8. 14
4. 11 9. 13
5. 16

p. 26
1. 2 Remainder = 1
2. 3 Remainder = 1
3. 6 Remainder = 3
4. 5 Remainder = 0
5. 6 Remainder = 2
6. 13 Remainder = 1

p. 27
Number Problems
1. 105 6. 21
2. 78 7. 15
3. 234 8. 14
4. 378 9. 9
5. 144   Remainder: 2
    10. 25

Word Problems
1. 24 books
2. 65 books

p. 29
1. $\frac{5}{6}$
2. $\frac{2}{9}$
3. $\frac{5}{5}$
4. $\frac{5}{12}$
5. $\frac{9}{10}$
6. $\frac{2}{4}$

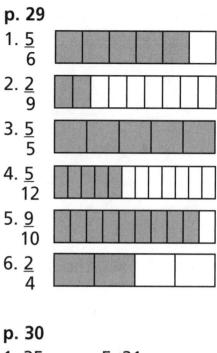

p. 30
1. $\frac{35}{50}$ 5. $\frac{21}{20}$
2. $\frac{3}{22}$ 6. $\frac{54}{100}$
3. $\frac{15}{15}$ 7. $\frac{35}{40}$
4. $\frac{39}{80}$ 8. $\frac{2}{35}$

p. 31
1. $3\frac{2}{4}$ cups of sugar and flour
2. $9\frac{3}{5}$ miles

p. 32
1. $\frac{14}{100}$ 4. $\frac{80}{100}$
2. $\frac{11}{100}$ 5. $\frac{24}{100}$
3. $\frac{18}{100}$

47

p. 33
Mixed Numbers

1. 5 $\frac{5}{6}$ 4. 1 $\frac{3}{12}$

2. 4 $\frac{2}{4}$ 5. 13 $\frac{7}{8}$

3. 7 $\frac{9}{10}$

Percentages

1. $\frac{50}{100}$ 3. $\frac{35}{100}$

2. $\frac{75}{100}$ 4. $\frac{92}{100}$

p. 35

p. 36

1. 0.5   6. 1.2
2. 0.5   7. 0.1
3. 0.7   8. 0.6
4. 0.6   9. 0.3
5. 0.6   10. 0.9

p. 37

1. 1.7   6. 9.9
2. 5.3   7. 3.4
3. 2.9   8. 7.8
4. 8.1   9. 2.5
5. 4.6   10. 8.2

p. 38

1. 7.8   6. 8.1
2. 3.2   7. 2.7
3. 8.9   8. 8.2
4. 2.1   9. 1.9
5. 9.7   10. 8.1

p. 39
Decimals and Mixed Numbers

1. 1.7   3. 0.3
2. 0.5   4. 6.2

Adding and Subtracting Decimals Greater Than 1

1. 8.8   4. 1.7
2. 3.2   5. 9.1
3. 5.4

p. 41

1. D.
2. C.
3. A.
4. C.
5. D.

p. 42

1. =   3. <
2. >   4. >

p. 43

1. $3.45
2. $5.85
3. $9.95
4. $14.15
5. $14.21
6. $27.22

p. 44

1. $5.00
2. $1.25
3. $2.71
4. $10.55
5. $7.35

p. 45

1. $2.85
2. $15.95
3. $33.22
4. $3.25
5. $0.83
6. $1.47